BUS OPERATORS 1970
The South-East and Eastern Counties of England

Gavin Booth

Ian Allan PUBLISHING

Contents

First published 2005

ISBN 0 7110 3032 4

All rights reserved. No part of this book may be reproduced or transmitted in any form or by any means, electronic or mechanical, including photocopying, recording or by and information storage and retrieval system, without permission from the Publisher in writing.

© Ian Allan Publishing Ltd 2005

Design by Hieroglyph

Published by Ian Allan Publishing

An imprint of Ian Allan Publishing Ltd, Hersham, Surrey KT12 4RG

Printed by Ian Allan Printing Ltd, Hersham, Surrey KT12 4RG

Code: 0509/B2

Visit the Ian Allan Publishing website at www.ianallanpublishing.com

Previous page: Several of the operators featured in this book had turned to 36ft-long dual-door single-deckers to allow the speedier adoption of driver-only operation. This is a Lowestoft Corporation AEC Swift 2MP2R, new in 1969 with Eastern Coach Works 45-seat bodywork built in the same town.
Tony Wilson

This page: Other municipal fleets in the area stuck mainly with double-deckers during the 1960s, but bought batches of single-deckers in the 1970s. This Colchester Corporation Leyland Atlantean PDR1/1 with Massey body still had a conductor when photographed shortly after delivery in 1967.
R Nicholas Collins

Facing page: London Transport still had nearly 3,000 RT family double-deckers in its fleet in 1970, the newest delivered in 1954 and the last examples placed in service in 1958/9. An RT sits at Bexleyheath garage early in 1971, parked beside an LT roundel.
Tom Maddocks

Front cover: When the former Country Area services were transferred to the National Bus Company in 1970, London Transport still retained over 6,000 buses, including nearly 3,000 RTs like RT1063, seen at Orpington on the fringe of the GLC area.
Tony Wilson

Back cover, upper: On the south coast at Bexhill, a Maidstone & District 1967 Leyland Panther with Willowbrook body.
Ted Jones

Back cover, lower: Lowestoft Corporation specified locally built Eastern Coach Works bodywork for its 1969 AEC Swifts.
Tony Wilson

Introduction

When I started researching this book, the first of a new series, I quickly realised just how significant the year 1970 was. The fact that it begins a new decade is purely coincidental on this occasion – what matters is that it catches the British bus industry at the crossroads of two distinct eras.

In the year 1970 various important developments came together. Under a Labour government the National Bus Company had been formed in 1969 to unite the Tilling and BET groups, and the first fruits of this union were being seen. Control of the Scottish Bus Group was returned to Scotland in 1969 with the formation of the Scottish Transport Group. Over the autumn/winter of 1969/70, bus services in four of Britain's major conurbations were brought under the control of Passenger Transport Authorities, a move that would have far-reaching effects on NBC's operations in these areas. And in London the Greater London Council assumed control of the buses in its area, leaving the Country Area and Green Line networks to be picked up by a new NBC company, London Country.

This first book covers the area to the east of a fairly straight line drawn from The Wash to The Solent, providing a natural grouping of operators – the Tilling fleets in East Anglia, London Transport and London Country, the BET fleets in the south-east corner and the two very different territorial companies west of London. And there are the municipal operators, from Lowestoft to Portsmouth, and the independents, particularly in East Anglia.

Within this area are some of Britain's most charismatic and popular companies, like London Transport and Southdown, as well as a varied selection of municipalities and companies newly grouped under the NBC umbrella that were facing the realities of 1970 life, including the inexorable spread of car ownership, which was affecting the south-east rather more than other parts of Britain.

In this series I am looking at bus operators, notably the state-owned and local authority-owned companies, as well as the larger and more significant independents. Although I started out looking for suitable photographs taken strictly in 1970, this proved difficult, so the illustrations reflect buses that were – or at least could have been – seen in use with these operators in these liveries in 1970.

Gavin Booth
Edinburgh

A 1970 south-east snapshot

This series of books is designed to provide a snapshot of Britain's buses as they were in 1970, when the industry was very much at the crossroads. We start in south-east England which, for the purposes of this volume, draws a straight line from The Wash to The Solent and covers the bus operators to the right of this line.

What you get is a remarkably varied slice of England, dominated inevitably by London, the focal point for much of the economy of the area, and the principal destination for major longer-distance transport links.

But at the extremities you have north Norfolk, for instance. Not far from London these days with the direct electric train service to Kings Lynn, but often deeply rural in nature and worlds apart from London in so many ways. At the south-western end is Portsmouth and Southsea, the former an important naval base and ferry port next door to Southsea's tourist attractions. And right round the south-east coast there are some of England's best-loved seaside resorts – Brighton, Eastbourne, Margate, Southend-on-Sea, Great Yarmouth – many traditionally relying on weekend and high summer coach traffic from London, although these too were under threat from the private car, which brought so many more destinations within day trip distance for so many families.

State-owned bus companies provided much of the public transport in an area with a better network of rail services than the rest of Britain. In East Anglia, two former Tilling Group fleets dominated the scene, Eastern Counties and Eastern National, although there were still a number of significant independent operators, particularly in Suffolk and Essex, that complemented the operations of the territorial companies with services that linked more rural communities with the main market towns.

This, remember, was an era when deregulation of bus services wasn't even on the political agenda. Everything was regulated and operators jealously held on to their often hard-won service licences. Competition between bus operators didn't really exist, although there were places where services ran in parallel over lengths of route where passengers had a choice. Operators had to apply to the Traffic Commissioners to introduce brand-new routes, or even to change existing routes, and everybody from rival bus operators to local authorities to the state-owned British Rail had the right to object, a right that was frequently exercised.

The result was that bus networks changed less frequently than they do today, and sometimes the only way that operators could expand was to buy out a smaller company and its licences. Fares, too, were subject to formal applications and hearings; none of the quick-response fare cutting of the 21st century.

The area to the south of London was dominated by former BET Group companies, now part of the new NBC. Three of the best-known and best-loved BET fleets, East Kent, Maidstone & District and Southdown, provided the principal rural and interurban services in Kent and Sussex, as well as town services and longer-distance services, often to London. To the immediate west of London there was Thames Valley, a former Tilling fleet with regular services into London, as well as Aldershot & District, a BET company; in 1971 they would be merged as Alder Valley.

Within this south-east area there were 10 municipal operators; the creation of PTEs in other parts of England had reduced the number of municipal operators in the West Midlands, the north-west and Tyneside, but the south-east lacked any potential for PTEs on the 1960s model. Of course in a way London Transport was the first PTE, and it had been around since 1933.

The municipal operators were Brighton, Colchester, Eastbourne, Great Yarmouth, Ipswich, Lowestoft, Maidstone, Portsmouth, Reading and Southend.

And of course there was London, where the new Greater London Council had assumed control of the Central Area buses while NBC was wrestling to come to terms with London Country, a company that was steeped in London Transport culture, and which, by its very shape – a Polo Mint surrounding the Capital – would prove difficult to run; while most bus company areas had grown organically with boundaries that represented natural cut-off points, poor London Country had inherited a committee-designed camel of a company.

There were pockets of independent operation in the south-east, notably around Cambridge and Colchester, but here was an area that was largely dominated by the big players, NBC and London Transport. ∎

The former Tilling Group imposed much stricter vehicle standardisation on its fleets, a policy that would be adopted by the recently-formed National Bus Company. This Thames Valley Bristol Lodekka FLF6G of 1961 has 70-seat ECW bodywork, and is seen at Reading Stations.
Tony Wilson

1970
Changes all around

Why 1970? A good question. The British bus industry had come through the 1960s without much in the way of dramatic change. The structure of the industry had been largely unchanged for around 20 years, but it was an industry in decline as passenger numbers continued to plummet after the heady days of the early 1950s. Everyone knew why this was happening – the spread of private motoring meant that people were less reliant on public transport, and the television revolution changed people's leisure habits; now they preferred to stay at home in the evenings, and if they went out, well there was a British-built family car sitting outside. They knew why it was happening, but they didn't seem to know what to do about it.

Work patterns too were changing. Traditionally, many people worked in town and city centres, or were part of a large workforce at an industrial site. With the closure and run-down of many factories, and the move away from town centre working to new offices on the edge of town, it became more difficult and costly for bus companies to provide adequate services at the busiest times of day. Shift patterns, too, were changing as more workers rebelled against unattractive shifts and weekend work, which affected not only the services provided by bus companies but also the availability of drivers, conductors and mechanics.

Bus company managers knew what was happening, and while some seemed powerless to do anything about it, others were working hard to stem the passenger drift. Cutting costs to match declining revenue was important, and during the 1950s high-capacity lightweight buses that carried more passengers and consumed less fuel were widely used, but the size and shape of buses changed dramatically in the 1960s, cancelling out some of the benefits.

A major part of any bus company's costs was staff wages, and with over 240,000 staff employed in the British bus industry in 1970, and a fleet of around 74,000 vehicles, the collective wage bill was affecting the viability of services. Expressed as staff per vehicle – London Transport employed 6.0, municipal operators 4.02, National Bus Company 3.85 and private operators 1.3.

Leyland's Atlantean and Daimler's Fleetline had grown in importance during the 1960s as operators accepted that rear-engined double-deckers offered many advantages, including a seating capacity of up to 78 and the ability to operate them without a conductor. With the agreement of the trade unions driver-only operation of single-deckers with up to 45 seats had been possible since 1960, which had led many operators to switch to single-deckers in the mid-1960s. Then in 1966 driver-only double-deckers were legalised, even though some operators were sceptical about the ability of a single man – and it usually was a man at that time – to handle both a large bus and 80-plus passengers. And that was before the trade unions became involved. They, naturally, were concerned about the jobs that would be lost as conductors became redundant, and where driver-only operation was acceptable the unions tried to ensure that drivers were properly rewarded.

National Bus Company's newly-created London Country subsidiary faced the huge task of replacing its inheritance of older London Transport types – over 900 of its start-up fleet of 1,267 were RF and RT types conceived in a very different world. Three RF type Metro-Cammell-bodied AEC Regal IVs at Hertford bus station in 1971.
Tony Wilson

Under NBC the former Tilling Brighton Hove & District company found itself in common ownership with the former BET Group Southdown company and in 1969 BH&D was merged into Southdown, although the operations were separated again prior to privatisation in 1985. This ECW-bodied Bristol RESL6G was ordered by BH&D, was diverted to the main Southdown fleet in 1970, but a few months later had appeared in BH&D red/cream.
M P M Nimmo

Driver-only double-deckers came not a moment too soon for the bus industry and gave several operators the opportunity to catch their breath, but something more significant would have to be done to stem and even reverse the decline.

And that's when the government stepped in to restructure a significant part of Britain's bus industry.

The most significant changes were to the structure of the industry, a structure that had survived largely unchanged since the spread of state ownership in the late 1940s. For 20 years the bus industry had consisted of four main sectors. There was the state-owned sector controlled by the Transport Holding Company (THC), consisting mainly of the Tilling Group, the Scottish Bus Group and London Transport. At the end of 1968 this sector accounted for 34,000 of Britain's 74,000 buses because the privately-owned BET Group had finally agreed to sell its UK bus interests to THC. Then there was the municipal sector, just under 100 corporations running roundly 18,000 buses, trolleybuses and trams. And there was the independent sector, which included everything from significant bus operators like Lancashire United to one-coach private hire operators.

Under the government's plans only the independent sector would escape without any change.

What was done from 1968 onwards was, inevitably, politically-driven. As we have seen, something had to be done, but what was done resulted from the return of a Labour government to power in 1964. Before the Conservatives swept them out of office in 1951, Labour had engineered the Tilling and Scottish groups into state-ownership, along with London Transport and the railways, and had started to lay plans for area transport boards. The outcome of the 1951 election put the area boards on hold and there was a feeling that buses were fairly far down the political agenda. Then Prime Minister Harold Wilson appointed Barbara Castle as his Minister of Transport and

things really started to move. In effect Labour was taking things up where they had left off 13 years previously.

Area Boards, now Passenger Transport Authorities (PTAs), were resurrected, and the 1968 Transport Bill proposed four initial PTAs, around Birmingham, Liverpool, Manchester and Newcastle. The 20 municipally-owned fleets in the PTA areas would automatically be subsumed into the new bodies. The PTAs were the policy-makers and would operate through Passenger Transport Executives (PTEs).

It was partly the spectre of compulsory takeover of some of its most lucrative companies, which operated in PTA areas, that led the BET Group to sell its bus interests to the Transport Holding Company in November 1967. This in turn paved the way for the creation of a new state-owned bus giant, National Bus Company (NBC), which from 1 January 1969 would control all the former Tilling and BET bus interests in England and Wales – more than 20,000 buses. At the same time, the new Scottish Transport Group transferred control of the Scottish Bus Group (SBG) back to Scotland and threw in the railway-owned Caledonian Steam Packet Company. Control of London's Central Area buses passed to the recently-formed Greater London Council (GLC) on 1 January 1970, at the same time that a new NBC company, London Country Bus Services Ltd, gained control of the former Country Area and Green Line network that surrounded the GLC area.

London Transport received substantial deliveries of rear-engined AEC Merlin and Swift single-deckers between 1966 and 1972 before reverting to double-deckers. They would have short lives in London service. A new Park Royal-bodied Swift is seen at Edgware in July 1970.
M A Penn

So now around two-thirds of Britain's buses and coaches were in public ownership – some 50,000 of them. NBC represented nearly half of that total, with London Transport and the four new PTEs accounting for a further quarter, and the balance operated by the remaining municipal fleets and SBG.

Another significant provision in the 1968 Transport Act was the introduction of the Bus Grant scheme, which allowed operators to claim back 25% of the cost of new buses that met certain criteria – essentially that they were suitable for driver-only operation. The intention here was to encourage operators to update their fleets, and most operators needed no second bidding, particularly when the grant went up to 50%.

Unfortunately, there wasn't a range of reliable models waiting in the wings. There weren't even many chassis manufacturers as a result of Leyland's remarkable growth in the 1960s which had seen the acquisition of most of the competition – AEC, Bristol, Daimler and Guy in particular – and found itself as the cornerstone of a giant manufacturer, the British Leyland Motor Corporation (BLMC), which not only controlled most of Britain's bus and truck manufacture, but also the bulk of its car industry – Austin, Morris, Rover and Triumph.

Until 1969 the bus side of BLMC had been churning out front-engined double-deckers like the AEC Regent V, Bristol Lodekka, Daimler CV and Guy Arab, but Bus Grant put paid to them. And its main rear-engined double-deck models, the Daimler Fleetline and Leyland Atlantean, had been conceived in the late 1950s and many operators were finding them irritatingly troublesome, notably the Atlantean. A reworked Atlantean was in the system, but wouldn't appear until 1972.

The single-deck range was equally mixed. There were trusted favourites like the AEC Reliance and Leyland Leopard, but there were mid-1960s models like the AEC Swift and Leyland Panther, rushed out to satisfy a demand for urban buses suitable

for driver-only operation but proving to be less than reliable in the hands of several operators. Again Leyland was working on a new model that was intended to solve these problems but in the meantime driver-only double-deckers were legalised and many of the operators who had switched to driver-only single-deckers in the mid-1960s switched back to double-deckers as soon as they could.

So 1970 was the year when the bus industry was thrown up in the air only to come down to earth in a very different form. True, it would be a couple more years before bus passengers saw much change to their local NBC buses; they still wore their standardised Tilling and more individual BET liveries and only the more observant passengers would notice that Tilling's buying policy was starting to creep into BET fleets. The new, smaller, London Transport Executive (LTE) continued much as before, but London Country faced a huge task in its vast 'mint-with-a-hole' area surrounding London with a potential clash of the very different London Transport and NBC cultures. There was little immediate change to SBG's buses but the four new PTEs worked hard to establish their identities in their new role in four of England's busiest conurbations.

In 1970 buses and coaches in Britain were still carrying nine billion passengers annually, and if this sounds like an impressive figure, remember that it had been dropping steadily since the early 1950s. But even if passenger figures seemed to be in freefall, they should be viewed in the context of other modes of transport. Buses and coaches, for instance, still carried more than ten times as many passengers as Britain's railways, although both modes were steadily losing out to private motoring. In 1954 buses and coaches accounted for 38% of passenger transport, expressed in passenger kilometres, with railways on 18% and private motoring on just 35%. By 1970 private motoring was up to 76%, while buses and coaches had dropped to 14% and railways to 9%.

Of the nine billion-plus journeys in 1970, NBC, London Transport and the four PTEs accounted for nearly three-quarters of these, followed by municipal operators (15%), Scottish Bus Group (5%) and private operators (6%).

Although the events of the late 1960s heralded the start of a decade of relative stability, everything was thrown up in the air again in the 1980s, when a different shade of political dogma unpicked much of the 1968 Act. And it's probably true to say that since 1970 things have rarely been boring in the British bus industry. ∎

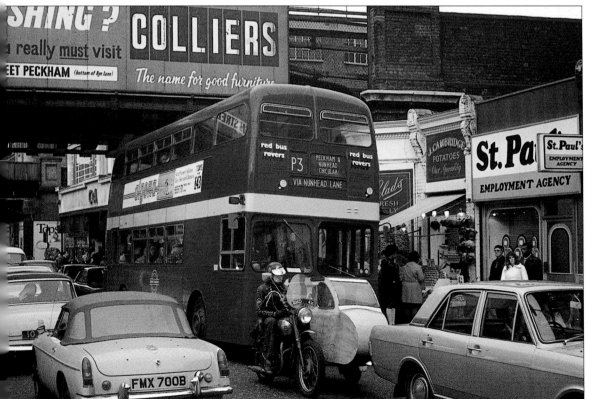

Above: Although Lowestoft Corporation bought big single-deckers from 1969, its small fleet included traditional rear entrance halfcab double-deckers like this 1967 Leyland Titan PD2/47 with 62-seat Massey body.
Tony Wilson

Left: Traffic congestion has been a problem in London for many years, as this busy scene demonstrates. One of London Transport's 47 Leyland Atlantean PDR1/1 with Park Royal bodies, new in 1965, is caught in Rye Lane on the P3 Peckham and Nunhead Circular service.
Tony Wilson

The eastern counties

In our broad definition of the south-east, we start in East Anglia, an area dominated by two Tilling Group fleets, Eastern Counties and Eastern National. With most of their fleets made up of standard-issue Tilling fare, products of in-house manufacturers Bristol and Eastern Coach Works (ECW), one was a red Tilling fleet, the other a green one.

The northern tip of the area, Norfolk, boasted one substantial company operator and one municipal operator.

The aptly-named Eastern Counties Omnibus Company was headquartered at Norwich, with, in 1970, a fleet of 765 buses, a fairly even mix of single- and double-deckers, plus 70 coaches. All the fleet figures quoted are from the 1970/71 edition of 'The Little Red Book', an invaluable source of information and a publication that is still published annually.

The Eastern Counties Omnibus Co Ltd (ECOC) was formed in 1931 to bring together four important operators that had set up in different parts of Norfolk, Suffolk and Cambridgeshire. In the late 1920s the London & North Eastern Railway (LNER) bought substantial interests in the Ipswich-based Eastern Counties Road Car and the vast United Automobile empire, and LNER with the London Midland & Scottish railway company (LMS) bought into Peterborough Electric Traction and the Cambridge-based Ortona companies.

The new Eastern Counties set about buying up independent

The nature of the territory served by Eastern Counties has meant that it has often had a fairly elderly fleet and has regularly received buses cascaded from other companies in the same ownership. This 1954 Bristol LS5G with 45-seat ECW body, seen in Great Yarmouth in June 1970, is one of 13 acquired from its southern neighbour, Eastern National, in 1966. It displays the typically helpful Eastern Counties style of destination display.
Ted Jones

Also in Great Yarmouth in June 1970, but in its last few months with Eastern Counties, a 1954 Bristol KSW5G with normal-height ECW 60-seat body, again displaying a less than helpful destination. This had been ECOC's last K type delivery before the company moved on to the Bristol Lodekka.
Ted Jones

under ECOC control until ECW was formed in 1937.

The 1970 ECOC fleet included over 200 Bristol Lodekkas, the shorter LD and FS models with five-cylinder Gardner 5LW engines rather than the more common and more powerful six-cylinder 6LW, a reflection of the flat terrain served on the company's routes. Older Bristol double-deckers, most with 5LW engines, were K type variants including the wider, longer KSW. These too had ECW bodies, a mix of highbridge buses for urban work and lowbridge buses for interurban and more rural work.

The single-deck bus fleet included front-engined Bristol Ls, underfloor-engined LSs and MWs, and rear-engined REs, in bus, dual-purpose and coach form. Again the Gardner 5LW was the engine of choice, although later MW coaches had 6HLW engines and this was standard on the larger REs.

For lighter duties ECOC was a major operator of the lightweight Bristol SC4LK, again with ECW bodywork, the majority fitted out for bus work although there was one batch of SC coaches.

During 1970 ECOC took further deliveries of Bristol's lightweight underfloor-engined LH model, including shorter-length buses that had been ordered by Luton Corporation, but diverted following the acquisition of the municipal business by neighbouring NBC company, United Counties. Also in 1970 came deliveries of the Bristol RELL and the recently-introduced

operators, including the Norwich Electric Traction company, operating trams and buses. These acquisitions put ECOC in a very strong position as a major territorial operator covering Norfolk, Suffolk and Cambridgeshire, with 17 principal garages plus numerous smaller outstations. It dominated Norfolk and spread well beyond the county boundaries, south to Ipswich, and east to Peterborough and Cambridge.

From 1935 the ECOC fleet had been mainly of Bristol/ECW manufacture, and when the Tilling Group passed into state ownership under the British Transport Commission in 1948, the Bristol/ECW combination became standard for all Tilling fleets. The ECW factory in Lowestoft, in Eastern Counties territory, had its roots in the United bodyworks there, and continued

Left: Another secondhand acquisition, a former United Counties Bristol LS6G coach in the Eastern Counties Cambridge garage.
Gavin Booth

Below: At Colchester on express duties in August 1970, a newly-delivered Eastern Counties Bristol RELL6G with 50-seat ECW dual-purpose body in the cream/maroon coach livery.
W T Cansick

with electric trams at the beginning of the 20th century, introducing motorbuses in the 1920s and abandoning its trams in 1933.

Although small (61), the Great Yarmouth fleet offered a variety of double-deck types, including AECs and Leylands with Massey bodies, Daimler CVG6s with Roe forward entrance bodies, Leyland Atlanteans with Metro-Cammell and Roe bodies, including some unusual 28ft-long examples, and Fleetlines with Roe bodywork. The single-deck fleet was equally varied – eight Daimler Freelines with Roe bodies, six AEC Reliances with Pennine bodies and three rare Leyland Atlanteans with Marshall single-deck bodies. In 1970 it bought 10 new AEC Swifts with two-door Willowbrook bodies, and would go on to buy more Swifts in the 1970s. These replaced Leyland Titans.

rear-engined VRT double-decker; ECOC went on to build up a substantial VRT fleet.

Withdrawals in 1970 included Bristol Ks, including the company's last K5G, as well as SCs and the last of its LS4Gs with four-cylinder Gardner engines.

The rump of Eastern Counties survives as First Eastern Counties, with some 400 buses, but operating in a more restricted area following the creation of Cambus in the lead-up to deregulation and privatisation. Although both ECOC and Cambus were initially bought from NBC by management teams, subsequent sales brought them into the big groups – ECOC to GRT Bus Group in 1994, Cambus to Stagecoach in 1995.

Within ECOC territory were two seaside municipalities. Great Yarmouth Corporation had started, like so many others,

In 1996 the Great Yarmouth Transport company was acquired by FirstBus and branded Blue Bus.

The other seaside municipal fleet was Lowestoft Corporation, with just 16 buses in 1970. The corporation had introduced an electric tram route in 1903 and the trams were replaced by buses in 1931. Britain's most easterly municipal operator had bought AEC Regents in the postwar years, moving on to Leyland Titans in the mid-1960s. Locally-built ECW bodes were favoured as long as these were generally available, and, like the other East Anglia municipalities, Lowestoft favoured Massey bodies, although it also bought East Lancs bodies for its Leylands. In 1969 it returned to ECW for bodies on four AEC Swifts, and would go on to buy more. In 1970 it bought two of Great Yarmouth's Pennine-boded AEC Reliances. Withdrawn in 1970

Above: At least this 1965 Bristol MW5G with 45-seat ECW body, seen in Beccles, is displaying a helpful destination. The MW succeeded the LS in the Bristol/ECW catalogue.
Tony Wilson

Left: From 1966 Eastern Counties turned to the longer Bristol Lodekka FLF6G model with 70-seat ECW bodywork, represented by this 1967 example in service in Cambridge. This bus, with 15 others, went north to Western SMT in 1973, receiving Bristol/ECW VRTs in return as part of the famous National Bus Company/Scottish Bus Group exchange.
Geoff O'Brien

were elderly ECW-bodied AEC Regent IIs.

Renamed Waveney District Council Transport in 1974, Eastern Counties acquired its operations in 1976/7.

Another municipal operation in Eastern Counties area was Ipswich Corporation, which had moved quickly from trams to trolleybuses in the 1920s and, unusually, operated no motorbuses until 1950. Within a few years trolleybus replacement started and was completed in 1963. Ipswich favoured AEC motorbuses through the 1950s and 1960s, but moved on to the Leyland Atlantean in 1968, this batch carrying ECW bodies. Like several municipal operators Ipswich was converting its Atlanteans for driver-only operation in 1970. Six Willowbrook-bodied AEC Swifts were ordered during the year. In 1970 Ipswich operated 72 buses; Ipswich Buses is still in local authority ownership and today runs a fleet of around 90 buses.

South of Eastern Counties was the other major Tilling Group operator in East Anglia, Chelmsford-based Eastern National Omnibus Company, with an area centred on Essex, but stretching into Suffolk and Hertfordshire. Although its roots were in the National Steam Car Company, Eastern National came into existence in 1930, covering a wider area that included Bedfordshire. Following the sale of the Tilling Group to the state, Eastern National territory underwent major changes; it lost its local routes in Grays, Essex, to London Transport in 1951 and in 1952 its Midland area was transferred to United Counties.

Above: **Representing later generations of Bristol/ECW single-deckers in the Eastern Counties fleet, a 1969 RELL6G with 43-seat ECW body in Southwold with an LH6P 45-seater in the background. Although LHs first appeared in the fleet in 1968, this is a 1971 example.**
Tony Wilson

Left: **Eastern National built up a substantial fleet of Bristol/ECW Lodekkas. This early LD5G example, dating from 1954, was still in service in Southend in 1972. It had started life with Eastern National's associated Westcliff-on-Sea fleet.**
Tony Wilson

Its 1970 operating area was concentrated in Essex, but stretched north to meet with Eastern Counties and west with London Transport. It had 16 garages, including one in Wood Green, London.

Since the mid-1930s most Eastern National buses had been Bristols, and in 1970 these included LS, MW and RE single-deckers, and KSW, LD, LDL, FS and FLF double-deckers. Like its northern neighbour, Eastern Counties, it favoured five-cylinder Gardner engines for most of its service buses through the 1950s. Deliveries during 1970 included further batches of RELL buses and RELH coaches, including some with Duple Commander bodywork. Withdrawals included KSW5Gs, all of its 1958/9 MW coaches and its last Bedfords.

There were 665 buses and coaches in the Eastern National

fleet in 1970, and its present-day successor, First in Essex, has just 180 vehicles.

In Eastern National territory were just two municipalities. Southend Corporation started with electric trams in 1901 and gradually replaced these with trolleybuses; Southend became an all-motorbus fleet in 1954. A co-ordination agreement was made in 1955 with Eastern National and its then subsidiary, Westcliff-on-Sea Motor Services, which led to joint operation of local services in and around the borough.

The 82-strong 1970 fleet was dominated by Leylands, single-deck Leopards and ex-Glasgow Worldmasters, plus Titans with lowbridge bodies; there were also lowheight AEC Bridgemasters and Leyland-Albion Lowlanders. In the 1970s Southend moved on to Leyland-engined Daimler Fleetlines. During 1970 it

converted its Lowlanders to driver-only operation and withdrew its long-lived Daimler CWA6 open-toppers as well as the first of a batch of Albion Aberdonians. Southend Transport was purchased by British Bus in 1993, and services are now provided by the local Arriva company.

The other Essex municipality was Colchester Corporation, which like so many others started with electric trams in the early 20th century, moving on to motorbuses in the 1920s.

The 1970 Colchester fleet consisted of 45 buses, mainly AEC and Leyland double-deckers with Massey bodies, though Massey-bodied Atlanteans were bought in 1967/8. Colchester would go on to buy more Atlanteans as well as Bristol RELLs in the 1970s. Acquired in 1970 was an ex-Hedingham & District

AEC Reliance/Plaxton, the first single-decker bought for the fleet for nearly 40 years. During the year the corporation also fitted platform doors to some of its Titans, but not heaters! The Colchester municipal bus operation was bought by British Bus in 1993 and although it has been part of the Arriva network, in 2004 it was sold to Tellings-Golden Miller.

An unusual aspect of bus services in East Anglia in 1970 was the concentration of independent bus operators in certain areas. In the Cambridge area there were three famous names – Burwell & District, Premier Travel and Whippet.

Burwell & District started running buses in 1922, initially into Cambridge and later in the Soham and Bury St Edmunds areas. The fleet was dominated by Daimlers for many years, latterly

An Eastern National Bristol MW6G with the later style of ECW coach body at Bishops Stortford in 1969 after it had been converted to a 41-seat driver-only bus using seats from withdrawn Bristol KSWs and fitted with jack-knife doors.
R Nicholas Collins

One of two Bristol FS5G Lodekkas with 60-seat ECW bodies delivered to Eastern National in 1960 is seen in Southend on driver training duties.
R Nicholas Collins

Fleetlines, but also bought secondhand double-deckers including an AEC Renown prototype. The Burwell & District business passed to Eastern Counties in 1979.

Cambridge-based Premier Travel was set up in the 1930s and grew by expansion and acquisition to become a significant operator of local and longer-distance services. The local bus fleet was largely stocked with secondhand buses, including double-deckers, but new coaches were bought, and AEC Reliances with Alexander Y type bodies were favoured for a number of years. Premier Travel's bus and coach business was sold to AJS Group in 1988 and most of it was sold on again to Cambus two years later.

Whippet Coaches of Hilton, Huntingdonshire, is still in business. It started in 1919 and developed a network of services in the Cambridge, Huntingdon and St Ives areas using single-deck and double-deck vehicles, many bought new.

Equally famous were the services provided by a range of Suffolk-based operators in their local areas and into Colchester. Most had small fleets, typically 10 or fewer vehicles including private hire coaches, and inspired great local loyalty among their passengers. Two larger operators based in Essex were Osborne of Tollesbury and Hedingham & District. Osborne, a long-established family-owned business mainly operating into Colchester, had a famously varied fleet of over 40 vehicles that in 1970 included AEC Bridgemasters and a Renown, in addition to the more staple fare of AECs and Bedfords. Hedingham & District was a newer operation, running 20 buses on routes that included joint operations with Eastern National into Colchester. The Hedingham business survives today and has grown dramatically since deregulation to a fleet of over 100 vehicles. ■

Left: Displaying a later style of Eastern National fleetname in 1972, a 1964 Bristol/ECW Lodekka FLF6B at Colchester bus station.
Mark Page

Below: A well-loaded 1969 Bristol RELL6G with 53-seat flat-screen ECW body is caught at Colchester bus station.
Photobus

Left: One of Eastern National's last Bristol/ECW Lodekkas, a 1967 FLF6G in cream/green livery with coach seating for the Southend-London service, seen here at Victoria Coach Station, London.
Geoff O'Brien

Below: Photographed on Great Yarmouth's Marine Parade in June 1970, a 1956 corporation AEC Regent V MD3RV with Massey 61-seat bodywork. The full destination display contrasted with the basic information provided on the local Eastern Counties buses.
Ted Jones

London-bound at Clacton in 1968 when it was brand-new, an Eastern National Bristol Lodekka FLF6G with coach seats and bright wheeltrims.
G R Mills

Eastern National received its first new batch of ECW-bodied Bristol VRTs in 1969; this one is seen at Colchester in 1971.
W T Cansick

In 1970 Lowestoft Corporation bought two of these AEC Reliance 2MU3RA with 39-seat Pennine bodies from Great Yarmouth.
M Fowler

Photographed the day before it first entered service in October 1969, one of Lowestoft's four AEC Swift 2MP2R with 45-seat ECW bodies at Rotterdam Road depot. Note the tramlines, a reminder of the 3ft 6in gauge system that closed in 1931.
G R Mills

Great Yarmouth was one of a number of municipal fleets in south-east England that favoured Wigan-built Massey bodywork, as on this 1957 Leyland Titan PD2/22 seen in July 1968.
G Mead

Unusual buses bought by Great Yarmouth Corporation in 1968 were three of these single-deck Leyland Atlantean PDR1//1s with Marshall 39-seat bodies.
M R Montano

Left: In 1964 Great Yarmouth Corporation bought two Leyland Atlantean PDR1/1 with 76-seat Roe bodies, and these carried names connected with the locally-set Charles Dickens novel, 'David Copperfield'.
Ted Jones

Below: The small Lowestoft Corporation fleet still included 1947-built AEC Regent IIs with locally-built ECW bodies in 1970. One of these is seen at the Harbour Bridge in June 1970, pursued by a considerably newer Eastern Counties Bristol RELL.
Ted Jones

Above: A rear view of a similar bus in Lowestoft reminds us that rear destination displays were also carried.

Ted Jones

Below: Ipswich Corporation's main deliveries in the 1960s were AEC Regent Vs with 65-seat bodies. This is a 1963 East Lancs-bodied example.

Tony Wilson

Above left: Ipswich Corporation's very first motorbuses, bought in 1950 when the cost of a trolleybus extension was seen as prohibitive, were AEC Regent IIIs with Park Royal bodies. These were still in service in 1970.
M A Penn

Above right: Ipswich turned to Leyland Atlanteans like this 1968 PDR1/1 example with ungainly ECW 74-seat bodywork, leaving White House Estate when new.
G R Mills

Left: After buying 'tin-front' Leylands, Southend specified the exposed-radiator PD3/4 model for its 1967 batch of three East Lancs-bodied rear entrance Titans.
G R Mills

Turning in Rayleigh High Street in 1968, a Southend Corporation Leyland Leopard PSU3/1R with 51-seat two-door East Lancs body, one of a batch of four delivered that year.
R Nicholas Collins

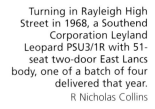

One of Southend's 1963 Alexander-bodied Leyland-Albion Lowlanders seen in 1970 fitted for driver-only operation; the projection to the left of the driver houses the ticket machine.
R Nicholas Collins

Colchester Corporation's first batch of Atlanteans were Massey-bodied PDR1/1s like this, though later deliveries had ECW bodies.
Leyland

Cambridge bus station offered interesting independent vehicles. In this view are a Premier Travel Leyland Titan PD2/3 with East Lancs body, formerly a Ribble 'White Lady' coach, and two Burwell & District buses, a Daimler Fleetline CRG6 with Willowbrook body, bought new in 1965, and the former demonstrator AEC Renown/Park Royal, 7552 MX.
Gavin Booth

Above: Southend's single-deck fleet included two of these early Leyland Leopard L1s with Weymann 43-seat dual-door bodies, complete with comprehensive destination display.
Tony Wilson

Below: 1970 was the last season for Southend Corporation's former Birmingham City Transport Daimler CWA6s, acquired in 1955 from Eastern National. This is a 1944 Duple-bodied example seen on Marine Parade in June 1970.
Omnicolour

Another independent with newer double-deckers at Cambridge was Whippet Coaches; this Leyland Atlantean PDR1/1 with Willowbrook 78-seat body was bought new in 1966.

Another view of AEC Renown/Park Royal demonstrator 7552 MX in the Burwell & District fleet. Renown demonstrator 8071 ML was sold to Osborne, Tollesbury.
G R Mills

During 1969/70 Premier Travel bought a number of these former Devon General 1957 AEC Reliances with Weymann 41-seat bodies, as seen at Drummer Street, Cambridge, in 1969.
G R Mills

For more than a decade Premier Travel favoured Alexander Y type-bodied AEC Reliances for its coach services. This one, at Clacton in 1967, was a new 11m-long 49-seater, but later deliveries were 12m 53-seaters.
G R Mills

Sitting at Osborne's Tollesbury garage in June 1970 are two Leyland Leopard PSU3A/4R with Willowbrook 53-seat bodies that had been ordered by Begg, Llantwit Fardre, but never reached Wales and were delivered direct to Essex.
G R Mills

W Norfolk of Nayland was one of the longest-established operators in the Suffolk/Essex area and this is a 1950 Austin CXB with Mann Egerton bodywork passing through its home village of Stoke by Nayland.
G R Mortimer

Left: Colchester Corporation favoured Massey bodywork in the 1950s and 1960s, and this is a 61-seat 1963 Leyland Titan PD2A/31 seen in later life carrying the simpler style of livery application.
Tony Wilson

Below: Osborne's, Tollesbury, had a good eye for secondhand double-deckers, like this 1963 former demonstrator AEC Renown 3B3RA/Park Royal 75-seater, seen in Colchester.
Mark Page

London and around

The south-east of England missed out on the major upheavals that followed the creation of the first four Passenger Transport Authorities (PTAs) in 1969/70 in the Midlands and north, but Britain's biggest bus operator, London Transport, was going through its most significant structural changes since the London Passenger Transport Board was set up in 1933.

The changes in the late 1960s came as a result of Harold Wilson's Labour government, and transport minister, Barbara Castle's energetic moves towards an integrated transport policy that produced legislation that created PTAs in the Tyneside, Greater Manchester, Merseyside and West Midlands areas, set up the National Bus Company in England and Wales and the Scottish Transport Group in Scotland, provided Bus Grants to encourage bus operators to renew their fleets with vehicles suitable for driver-only operation, among other provisions.

The Transport (London) Act dissolved the London Transport Board and vested responsibility for London Transport with the Greater London Council, working through the new London Transport Executive. Beyond Greater London the outer ring of services would be transferred to the new NBC, which set up a new company, London Country Bus Services Ltd, to operate these and the Green Line services that ran into and through central London.

London Transport had been around as an all-embracing transport authority since 1933 and had tackled the challenges of serving such a vast population in a methodical and often inspired way. Right from the creation of LPTB it had an inheritance of services that had little

Previous page: The classic RT type was still the most numerous class in Leyland Transport ownership, accounting for nearly half the fleet. This fine 1970 study shows RT1254 laying over at Ealing Broadway.
Mark Page

Top: Although it was converted to Routemaster operation in 1970, RTs still appeared on route 27. An RT passes an RM in Richmond in July 1971.
Tom Maddocks

Centre: Photographed in Whitehall on the 134, a late-model RML with offside illuminated advertisement panel on what looks like a hot July day.
G Mead

Left: The 33ft 5in-long SM class AEC Swifts with Marshall single-door 42-seat bodies entered service in 1970. On the first day Swifts were used in London service, 24 January, SM12 is at Catford Town Hall.
Edward Shirras

to do with what was being defined as Greater London, covering areas that were probably in the London job catchment area, but where the local economy was more closely related to towns in the counties around the Capital.

LT's Country Area routes reached out in a circle, starting in the north and moving clockwise, as far as Hitchin, Bishops Stortford, Brentwood, Sevenoaks, Tonbridge, East Grinstead, Horsham, Guildford, Woking, Windsor, Slough, High Wycombe, Aylesbury, Dunstable and Luton. Some of these routes linked with places in Greater London, but others had no real connection other than a historical one.

With the transfer of the routes in these areas to London Country on 1 January 1970, the LT bus fleet dropped by over 1,200 vehicles, and the new LTE was able to

Above: Park Royal issued this photo of an SMS in May 1970 when it announced in a press release headed 'London Built and London Bound' that it had won a contract for 870 buses 'for the Greater London area' – 275 Swifts like this, 367 Fleetline double-deckers, 90 36ft single-deckers (London Country's Green Line RP type AEC Reliance coaches), 48 33ft single-deckers (London Country's SM type AEC Swifts) and 90 30ft double-deckers (London Country's AN type Leyland Atlanteans).

Left: In London Transport's last few days in the Country Area, three Daimler Fleetlines were painted into a striking blue/silver livery for Stevenage Blue Arrow services. This one, with London Country fleetnames, was photographed at Stevenage on 17 December 1969. Edward Shirras

Below left: It would be some years before London Country could replace its inheritance of RTs with new and diverted driver-only buses. London Country

Below right: In July 1972 it was still possible to find LCBS RTs pressed into Green Line service, as here at Victoria. G F Walker

Left: RTs were to be found throughout LT territory, like RT1380 seen here at West Croydon ready to set off on its trek north to the Thames at Woolwich.
Murdoch Currie

Below: The last of the wide all-Leyland RTWs in the LT fleet, used latterly only on driver training duties, were withdrawn in 1970. RTW60 sits at Stonebridge Park garage.
Tony Wilson

Routemasters, right up to 1968, but the world had suddenly moved towards driver-only operation and RMs, however new, would never be suitable for this. LT's 1960s Reshaping Programme had come down firmly on the size of full-size single-deckers, hence the 500-plus Merlins and hundreds more of the shorter-length Swift that were on order. The trouble was, the world had then swung over to driver-only double-deckers after these were legalised in 1966 just as London's first Merlins were entering service; in fairness, driver-only double-deckers weren't even on the table when LT was formulating its forward plans. Other bus operators around the country switched from double-deckers to driver-only single-deckers in the 1960s to save on labour costs; indeed some stuck with single-deckers while others quickly returned to doubles. London, with the biggest fleet and the biggest commitment to single-deckers, was rather stymied until it could start to take in double-deckers at the levels it needed.

So in 1970 LT had a fleet that was still dominated by in-house designs like the RT, RM and RF, and a fleet-replacement programme that would cause much grief along the way. The 'off-the-peg' Merlins were proving to be troublesome but in a fast-changing world there wasn't the luxury of going back to the drawing-board, much as LT engineers would surely have preferred. The gestation time for the RM had been long – the first production examples entered service five years after prototype RM1 had first appeared – and there were several years of planning before that. The compromise was to buy buses that were essentially 'off-the-peg', but were in practice heavily Londonised.

At much the same time as the new London Transport Executive was settling in, the first of a fleet of Marshall-bodied

concentrate on serving the populous GLC area. This still left LT with more than 6,000 vehicles in its fleet – nearly 3,000 RT family double-deckers, virtually all 2,760 Routemasters less around 200 transferred to LCBS, 47 experimental Leyland Atlanteans, over 200 RF type AEC Regal IV single-deckers, over 500 of the newer AEC Merlins plus the fleet of Routemasters and the Executive Express AEC Reliances operated for British European Airways.

London's normally methodical fleet renewal policy had rather lost its way in the 1960s. Sure, it was still receiving one-door AEC Swifts was entering service, the SM type, followed by the two-door SMS version with Park Royal bodies. Deliveries of SM and SMS types continued throughout 1970, and there would ultimately be 700 in the LT fleet, though like their Merlin bigger brothers, they didn't enjoy a long London life and most had been withdrawn by 1980.

LT was not blind to driver-only double-deckers, though; it took its only suitable buses, the 47 remaining XA type Leyland Atlanteans, plus rear-engined Routemaster, FRM1, and fitted them with fareboxes to work from its Croydon and Peckham garages. It also dipped a tentative toe into the double-deck market with an order for 117 Daimler Fleetlines with Park Royal bodies and the first of these were built during 1970 and placed in service early in 1971. The class would eventually total 2,646 buses, delivered between 1970 and 1978.

At the other end of their lives, the last Leyland-built RTLs and RTWs were withdrawn from the training fleet, and even LT's three Routemaster prototypes, RM1-3, were withdrawn from the active fleet and placed on training duties. Although there were still some 3,000 RTs, overhauls stopped during 1970 and withdrawals started in earnest; the last RT had run in LT service by the end of the decade.

If LT had problems with its fleet, spare a thought for London Country. It inherited a gloriously mixed fleet in 1970 – the majority LT-designed types like RTs, RFs, Routemasters, and little Guy GSs, plus 17 lowbridge AEC Regent III RLHs, three Atlanteans, eight Fleetlines, various Merlins and 14 AEC Reliance coaches. Not a typical NBC fleet by any measure, and to make matters worse, because the Country Area and Green Line fleets had been overhauled at LT's dedicated works at Aldenham and Chiswick, LCBS lacked any kind of central workshop facility – although 'light overhauls' and repaints continued at Aldenham for a period. It was not a promising start.

The 'mint-with-a-hole' area around London that was inherited by LCBS was not the most promising bus country. It included many affluent areas where car ownership levels were well above the national average and a large proportion of the bus services

Top: **Although London Transport had invested heavily in single-deckers of the AEC Merlin/Swift families, it still had over 200 RF type AEC Regal IV/Metro-Cammell single-deckers dating from the early 1950s in the 1970 fleet. This is RF340 on the suburban 80A linking Tooting with Walton-on-the-Hill, in Surrey.**
Tony Wilson

Above: **The last Routemasters had only been built for London Transport in 1968, so in 1970 virtually all were in service with the LTE, except for those transferred into the new London Country fleet. This is RM1737, famously the first overall advertising bus in London when it received this Silexine Paints scheme in August 1969; it was repainted into fleet livery a year later.**
Michael Dryhurst

Left: The 65 forward entrance Routemasters built for British European Airways in 1966/67 and operated by London Transport between Heathrow Airport and West London Air Terminal were being painted into this BEA livery from 1969. BEA25 is seen in Comwell Road in September 1970 towing a baggage trailer. All 65 were bought by LT in 1975 and some were used in normal service.
Omnicolour

Below: Of the 50 Leyland Atlantean PDR1/1s with 72-seat Park Royal bodywork bought in 1965, all but three that were in the London Country fleet were fitted with fareboxes and used as driver-only buses in the Croydon and Peckham areas. XA42 is seen at East Croydon on the C3 New Addington express service; today this route is tram-operated.
Murdoch Currie

were unremunerative. Add to this a fleet that had been designed in a different era for different operating circumstances, and the lack of overhaul facilities, and NBC had to move fast to order new buses for this, its second biggest fleet. It received 138 AEC Swifts that had been ordered by LT – they were even numbered in the same series as the LT examples – and for 1971 it ordered 90 Leyland Atlanteans and 90 AEC Reliance Green Line coaches. These would allow more driver-only operation, which had reached 40% in 1970, but with rear entrance halfcab double-deckers accounting for more than half the fleet, there was a limit to what could be done in the short term.

Delivered to LCBS during 1970 were the first of the SM type Swifts with two-door bodies by Park Royal and Metro-Cammell, while withdrawals included RTs and the last of the RLHs, bringing the operation of lowbridge double-deckers to an end. Unlike LT, which withdrew Routemasters RM1-3 in 1970, LCBS put the fourth prototype, RMC4, back into service from Hatfield.

At first the only external changes were to the legal lettering, with LCBS registered at Bell Street, Reigate, Surrey, and LONDON COUNTRY gold fleetnames. A new symbol was quickly adopted, first for publicity and later on the vehicles. Nicknamed the flying wheelbarrow, it was said to represent 'the encircling of London by LCBS and the green fields beyond Central London, suggesting operation in the country'. The circle also suggested a wheel and movement. LCBS initially stuck to LT Lincoln Green/cream, but then adopted canary yellow in place of the cream.

The scale of the financial problems facing LCBS was underlined when it gave notice to seven local authorities late in 1970 that 83 services would be withdrawn unless financial assistance was forthcoming.

Much has happened to the companies serving London and its surrounding area since 1970. London Transport adopted a district structure in 1979 and became London Regional Transport in 1984; then in 1985 LRT created London Buses, which was divided into 11 operating units in 1988, a prelude to

Above: **London's Red Arrow flat-fare services were started with AEC Merlins fitted with Strachans standee bodies. XMS4, seen at Victoria Street in 1967, had been renumbered MBS4 with a farebox rather than the turnstiles in the Red Arrows.**
Ted Jones

Left: **The next generation of Red Arrow buses were the AEC Merlins with Metro-Cammell bodywork that appeared in 1969. MBA 533 is seen at Victoria in 1972, terminus of the 507 to Waterloo.**
Murdoch Currie

privatisation in 1994. Now London's buses are run by the groups that dominate the rest of Britain's bus industry – Arriva, First, National Express, Go-Ahead and Stagecoach – and the bus fleet has been transformed with the encouragement of London Mayor, Ken Livingstone. With the withdrawal of the last Routemasters scheduled for the end of 2005, the London bus fleet will be 100% accessible, a remarkable achievement. And if London didn't escape privatisation, it escaped deregulation in the 1980s by opting for a route franchising system where the competition is for the route contract rather than on the streets.

What was London Country hasn't fared so well. As part of the privatisation process in the mid-1980s, NBC was directed to split four of its largest companies prior to sale, so London Country was split four ways – North East, North West, South East and South West; the South East company later adopted the name Kentish Bus & Coach.

London Country (North West), based near Watford, was first to be sold, in January 1988 to its management team, followed a month later by Reigate-based London Country (South West), to Drawlane, and a month later Kentish Bus & Coach, based in Northfleet, went to Proudmutual. London Country (North East), based in Hertford, was the last NBC company to be sold, and went in April 1988 to Alan Stephenson's AJS Group. But that was only the start of the process.

AJS divided LCNE into two companies, Sovereign and County Bus & Coach, and fairly quickly sold off parts of the operation, the Stevenage part to Luton & District and much of the County business in 1990. In 1991 much of what was left of AJS, including operations in Yorkshire, were sold to a new company, Blazefield Holdings. More recently, Blazefield has concentrated its business in Yorkshire and sold the Sovereign business on.

In 1990 London Country (North West) was sold to another former NBC company, Luton & District, which in turn became part of British Bus in 1994. London Country (South West), which traded as London & Country, was part of the Drawlane group, which became British Bus in 1992. Proudmutual, owners of Kentish Bus, also sold out to British Bus in 1994, bringing much of the old London Country company back into common ownership.

The compulsory acquisition of so many businesses in 1933 meant that there were few independent operators surviving in the London Transport area. Three that operated in areas that LT had abandoned or didn't appear to want were Continental Pioneer, Elms Coaches and Golden Miller.

Continental Pioneer got involved in local bus operation following an LT platform staff overtime ban, taking over the abandoned route 235 running between Richmond and Richmond Hill in 1968 using a mix of buses including ex-Thames Valley Bristol LLs and ex-LT RFs.

In 1966 Bernard Cheek's Elms Coaches took over Harrow area route 98B, again following the overtime ban, using secondhand Bristol buses, and from 1971 the route was operated by Elmtree Coaches, again run by Bernard Cheek.

F G Wilder's Golden Miller business started running buses on a service from Feltham Station to Bedfont, in south-west London, later numbered 601, when it took over Tourist Bus Service; the route had been the first since World War 2 to start with LT's consent. Two further services, 602 Feltham-Shepperton Station and 603 Feltham-Hanworth, started in 1968; in 1970 the Walton-on-Thames to Walton Station service of Walton-on-Thames Motor Co, which had been running since 1923 and had somehow escaped when LPTB was formed in 1933, was taken over. Tellings Golden Miller survives today as a 180-bus operator based in part of the old Fulwell garage and running many LT contracts. ∎

At the 1970 Commercial Show MCW showed this AEC Swift 4MP2R two-door 41-seater, from a batch delivered from late 1970 to replace RT buses.
Gavin Booth

Left: Resting at Waterloo, MBA609 awaits its driver for a journey on the 505 to Marble Arch in 1971. Note the two-stream front entrance and the coin-in-slot symbols.
Tony Wilson

Below: The MB class AEC Merlins were for conventional driver-only operation in the suburbs, and later examples had 50-seat single-door bodies like MB375 in leafy suburbia at the Coney Hall terminus of the short 138 route from Bromley North station.
Tony Wilson

Above: Another MB class Merlin/Metro-Cammell, MB352 at Barnet working on the long 84 route that linked Arnos Grove and St Albans.
Tony Wilson

Below: The MBS Merlins were two-door standee buses with 32 seats and space for 34 standing. MBS229 at Ealing Broadway in 1970 on the local E1 service to Greenford.
Mark Page

Above: At 33ft 5in the SM/SMS class AEC Swifts were shorter than the 36ft Merlins. Two 1970-delivered Swifts, SMS86 and 65, sit at Edgware station. The SM was a one-door 42-seater with Marshall bodywork and the SMS a two-door 33-seater with Marshall, Metro-Cammell or, as here, Park Royal bodies.
Tony Wilson

Below: Delivered to LT in 1970, Swift SMS253 with Park Royal body is seen at East Croydon in 1972 on the 166 linking Thornton Heath and Purley.
Murdoch Currie

Above: London Country inherited 263 AEC Regal IV RF type buses and 150 RF coaches from London Transport when it was set up in 1970, the newest 16 years old. They were destined to keep going until LCBS could source suitable single-deckers, in some cases buses diverted from other NBC fleets. This is RF304, a 38-seat bus that had formerly been a Green Line coach, bound for Chesham on the 336 at Chenies.
Tony Wilson

Below: At Guildford, loading for Dorking, RF249 is a 37-seat bus, again formerly a Green Line coach. Note that the London Transport roundel has been painted over.
Photobus

Above: With the London Country legal lettering covering the London Transport name, RF189 is a 37-seat bus pressed into Green Line service on the long 716 to Hitchin.
Photobus

Below: RF618 at St Albans in 1972 shows how the yellow relief and fleetnames adopted by London Country brightened the basic livery.
Tony Wilson

The twin headlamps and broad waistband reveal that this is one of the RFs modernised in the 1960s for Green Line duties. RF101, working as a 304 bus at Whitwell, Hertfordshire, where it performed a three-point turn.
Ted Jones

A modernised RF200 with yellow relief band on Green Line 719 duties in Park Lane, London.
Photobus

Some London Country RFs survived to receive NBC leaf green, but as here with LCBS yellow relief.
Photobus

Above: **Modernised RF171 at London Victoria in 1972 in full Green Line rig with roof boards working the 708 from Hemel Hempstead to East Grinstead.**

Murdoch Currie

Left: **London Country's inherited double-deck fleet in 1970 was dominated by 484 RTs, a type designed decades before and arguably not ideal for winning new customers in the Home Counties. With only 11 of its inherited double-deckers suitable for driver-only operation, LCBS faced a major task if it was to restock its fleet with newer types. And in the meantime the RTs had to soldier on, like RT605, here pottering through Chalfont St Giles towards Langley in 1971.**

Tony Wilson

Above: The LCBS RTs looked more at home in urban landscapes like Croydon, where RT3461 is seen working on the 403 in 1975.
Ted Jones

Below: Another urban London Country RT, this time to the north of London at Watford Junction, on the 347 Hemel Hempstead-Uxbridge corridor.
Tony Wilson

Left: Carrying the 'flying wheelbarrow' logo, RT4202 in NBC days as evidenced by the National Holidays advertisement on the side and the front adverts encouraging people to use Green Line services to link with National Express routes throughout the country.
Photobus

Below: The West Croydon bus station roundel is a reminder of RT3693's roots, as is the Routemaster in the background. Again, house advertising dominates the side and front spaces – promoting the 7-shilling (35p) Green Rover tickets. The advert hoarding remind us of times when cigarette advertising was acceptable. The long 405 route ended up in Sussex.
Photobus

Above: Picking up a healthy load in Redhill on the 411, RML2332 also carries house adverts proclaiming 'Here comes a National bus' and promoting Green Rovers – 75p in 1976. It was one of the 100 RMLs allocated to LT's Country Area in 1965/66.

Mark Page

Below: RCL2258 in Croydon starting out on the long 405 service to Crawley. Bought as coaches for Green Line work in 1965, the RCLs were downgraded to bus duties in 1972 when the coach routes went over to driver-only operation.

Photobus

Above: The eight experimental Daimler Fleetlines with Park Royal bodies bought by London Transport in 1965 came to rest in the Country Area, and XF6 is seen here freshly repainted out of the Stevenage Blue Arrow livery, working on their usual haunt, the 424.
Photobus

Below: Included in London Transport's legacy to LCBS were two batches of AEC Merlins, built in 1967/68. MB107 with two-door Metro-Cammell body, is seen at Bucks Hill.
Tony Wilson

Above: London Transport attempted to start the updating of the Green Line coch fleet when it bought 14 of these Willowbrook 43-seat AEC Reliance 4U2RA in 1965. Although this busy manufacturer's photo was taken in Windsor when they were new, it illustrates one of the more unusual Green Line types. They lost this grey/green livery in favour of the normal Green Line scheme before they were transferred to London Country.
AEC

Left: Continental Pioneer used former LT AEC Regal IV RF types on its short 235 local service in Richmond.
Photobus

The first new Bristol bus bought by a London independent for many years was this LH6L with Plaxton body bought by Golden Miller, Feltham in 1970.
Gavin Booth

A former United Auto 1952 Bristol LS5G in service with Elms Coaches on the 98B.
Edward Shirras

The Ford Transit minibus revolution was still more than a decade away in 1970, but Thames Weald used this Ford Transit on its Tunnel Express route linking Romford, Dartford, Gravesend and Sevenoaks. It is seen at Sevenoaks station.
Edward Shirras

West of London

A Thames Valley Bristol Lodekka FLF6G swings out of High Wycombe bus station for Great Missenden.
Ian Allan Library

Above: A smartly-presented Thames Valley Bristol Lodekka LD6B that was transferred from the Lincolnshire fleet in 1970.
Photobus

Left: Running under the trolleybus wires in Reading in 1967, a 1961 Thames Valley Bristol Lodekka FLF6G with 70-seat ECW body.
Tony Wilson

The area around what has become known to developers as the M4 Corridor, due west of London, has never in recent years been what operators would regard as 'good bus country'. The geography and relative affluence of Berkshire and north Hampshire has caused problems for a succession of bus companies over the past few decades. Most of these companies are descended from the two long-standing territorial operators, now together in 1970 under the new National Bus Company.

The Thames Valley Traction Company was former in 1915 by the British Automobile Traction company to run services between Reading and Maidenhead and grew to become the territorial operator covering Berkshire, connecting with London Transport to the east, City of Oxford to the north, Wilts & Dorset to the south-west and Aldershot & District to the south-east.

With its head office in Reading and garages at Bracknell, Maidenhead, Newbury, Oxford, Reading and High Wycombe, Thames Valley operated a fleet of 370 buses and coaches in 1970, all Bristol/ECW types except for a handful of Bedford coaches, mostly for its Oxford-based South Midland subsidiary. Most standard-issue Bristol/ECW types were represented, including coach-seated Lodekka double-deckers for the London-Reading corridor.

Above: **One of the rare Bristol SUS4As with 30-seat ECW bodies transferred from Bristol Omnibus to Thames Valley, at work in Slough.** Tony Wilson

Left: **At Windsor, Thames Valley and London Country services met. In this 1971 scene, a late-model Thames Valley Bristol FLF6G climbs towards the edge of Windsor Castle displaying a less than informative destination.** Tony Wilson

New deliveries for Thames Valley in 1970 included ECW-bodied Bristol LHs, RELLs and VRTs, and somewhat rarer Duple Commander-bodied LH coaches. It also received secondhand Lodekkas, LSs and even SUS4As from other NBC fleets, as it had become something of a last resting-place for redundant vehicles. At the same time it was withdrawing a range of older types from its fleet – LWLs, LSs, SCs, KSWs and Bedfords.

Under NBC, South Midland was transferred to City of Oxford in 1971, the year Thames Valley and former BET neighbour, Aldershot & District, were merged to become Alder Valley. In 1986 Alder Valley was itself split into two companies, Alder Valley North and Alder Valley South, which almost returned the companies to the pre-1971 situation, and in 1987 they were sold,

The Berks Bucks Bus Company (trading as The Beeline, and formerly Alder Valley North) to Len Wright's Q Drive company and Alder Valley South to Frontsource Ltd. Q Drive later bought Alder Valley South and Alder Valley Engineering from Frontsource, re-uniting the elements of the company, but after a confident start, Q Drive sold off its bus-operating business to other major players. Bracknell-based First in Berkshire, with 115 buses, is the closest 2005 equivalent to the 1970 company.

The other major part when Alder Valley was set up in 1971 was the Aldershot & District Traction company; in 1970 A&D operated 290 buses in Hampshire, Surrey, Sussex and Berkshire. Based in Aldershot, with garages at Aldershot, Alton, Guildford, Hindhead and Woking, A&D had been a BET Group company, based on operations that started in the

Aldershot and Farnborough areas in 1906.

It grew around local services in Aldershot, Camberley, Farnborough, Guildford and Woking, with regular express services between Farnham and London as well as seasonal express services to coastal resorts in Sussex and Hampshire. The heavy presence of military establishments in the Aldershot and Farnborough areas also helped the company's profitability.

The A&D fleet was famously built around Dennis chassis, built within its operating area at Guildford, and in 1970 there were 137 Dennis, but an almost equal number of AECs, reflecting Dennis's on-off approach to bus manufacture in the 1950s and 1960s. By the time Dennis bounced back in the 1980s and 1990s, A&D was no more.

The Dennises in the A&D fleet in 1970 were the Loline double-deckers bought between 1958 and 1965 with Alexander, East Lancs and Weymann bodies, which was the biggest concentration of the Loline model anywhere and represented roundly half of the total production of this model.

New deliveries in 1970 were Marshall-bodied two-door Bristol RELL6Gs, introducing a new type to the fleet, and Duple Commander-bodied Reliances. Withdrawals included Lolines and Reliance buses.

A&D's post-1970 fate was largely tied up with its northern neighbour, Thames Valley. As recounted above, it was absorbed into the new Alder Valley company in 1971, then separated out for sale as Alder Valley South and later reunited with other parts of the Alder Valley empire under Q Drive. The former A&D Guildford and Woking operations were later sold to London & Country and became part of Arriva. The remains of A&D – Aldershot, Alton and Hindhead – went to Stagecoach, which operates it as Stagecoach Hants & Surrey as part of the Stagecoach South group.

Top: One of four Bristol RELH with Duple Commander III bodies operated by Thames Valley's associated fleet, South Midland, on the Reading-Heathrow link.
Ian Allan Library

Above: A 1969 Thames Valley Bristol VRTSL6G with 70-seat ECW body at Victoria Coach Station on the London-Reading route B.
Edward Shirras

The only municipal fleet in the area was Reading Corporation, which owned 109 buses in 1970, roughly two-thirds single-deckers. The corporation had become a horse tramway operator in 1901 and proceeded to convert it to electric traction, and between 1936-39 the trams were replaced by trolleybuses. Reading was an enthusiastic trolleybus operator, and its system was one of the last in the UK to close, in 1968. It was also an enthusiastic user of driver-only single-deckers, moving on to double-deckers when these became legal.

Its 1970 fleet included AEC, Bristol and Dennis types, the AECs being Regents and Reliances, the Bristols RELLs and the Dennises Lolines. During 1970 it ordered the first of a fleet of Northern Counties-bodied 'jumbo' 33ft-long Bristol VRTs.

Reading Transport is still in local authority ownership in 2005, with a fleet of 210 buses.

Bus-operating independents in the area west of London in 1970 included Chiltern Queens of Reading, operating AEC Reliance buses, Reliance Motor Services of Newbury, with 38 vehicles of AEC, Bedford and Ford manufacture, Safeguard, still operating in the Guildford area, Smith's of Reading, with 100 vehicles, mainly coaches but double-deckers for contract work, and Tillingbourne Valley, later Tillingbourne Bus Co. ∎

Above: Wearing the Aldershot & District livery of two shades of green with cream, complete with ornate fleetname, this AEC Reliance MU3RV was new in 1954 with a Strachans coach body but had been rebodied in the mid-1960s by Weymann when photographed at Reading Stations in 1967.
Tony Wilson

Below: With a reversed livery and simpler fleetname, a 1961 AEC Reliance with Weymann body at Godalming in April 1970.
Omnicolour

Left: Aldershot & District's first batch of 34 Dennis Lolines, bought in 1958, had East Lancs 68-seat bodies to this style, as seen at Hindhead in 1968.
Tony Wilson

Below: Although the photo was taken later in Alder Valley days this Dennis Loline III with 68-seat Alexander body from the 1962 batch of 37, is still in full A&D colours in Guildford in 1974.
Mark Page

Above: Aldershot & District's last batch of Dennis Lolines, delivered in 1964/65, had Weymann 68-seat bodies.

Edward Shirras

Opposite above: The long-established Guildford independent, Safeguard Coaches, ran this early 36ft AEC Reliance 2U3RA with Duple (Midland) 53-seat body.

Edward Shirras

Opposite: In Guildford in 1971 an ex-Western National Bristol LS/ECW on the Tillingbourne Valley service to Peaslake, using the former London Transport route number 448.

Edward Shirras

Left: From the late 1950s, Reading Corporation turned to two-door standee single-deckers in a big way, first on AEC Reliance chassis then Bristol RELL6G. This is one of the RELLs, a 1968 example with Pennine body seating 34 with space for 35 standees, at Reading Stations.
Photobus

Below: Reading's last new front-engined double-deckers were Dennis Lolines with East Lancs bodies bought in 1962/66. After that Reading concentrated on standee single-deckers before returning to double-deck purchases with Northern Counties-bodied Bristol VRTs from 1971. A 1962 Loline with a short reversed registration number in St Mary's Butts in 1973 followed by a Pennine-bodied Bristol RELL6G.
Ted Jones

The south-east coast

Above: For many, the classic postwar buses in the East Kent fleet were the Park Royal full-fronted AEC Regent Vs like this 1958 example. East Kent was one of a small number of BET Group fleets like Ribble and Southdown who specified full fronts for their forward entrance double-deckers.
Photobus

Below: The 'Queen Mary' Leyland Titan PD3s with full-fronted Northern Counties bodies in the traditional green/cream livery and fleetname, typified the Southdown fleet, and remain popular favourites with enthusiasts. This 1961 example is in service at Southsea.
Tony Wilson

Although former Tilling Group companies dominated the bus services in East Anglia in 1970, the former BET Group had a firm hold on England's south-eastern corner. Three important and charismatic fleets covered the coastal areas and the hinterland towards the fringes of the London Transport area, with four municipal operators providing local services.

Starting at the east of the area, in Kent, there was the East Kent Road Car company, based in Canterbury and covering the eastern tip of the county, taking in important resorts like Margate and Ramsgate, the ferry ports of Dover and Folkestone, and serving a substantial rural area in addition to these better-known operations.

The company was formed in 1916, an amalgamation of various pioneering operations in the area, and grew to become a substantial operator, with a fleet of 588 buses and coaches in 1970. AECs and Guys were favoured; there were AEC Reliance buses and coaches, AEC Regent V and Bridgemaster double-deckers, and Guy Arab double-deckers. Park Royal bodies had been favoured for many years and were fitted to many single-deckers and all of the double-deckers. Delivered in 1969 had been the first of three batches of AEC's rear-engined Swift, in this case with Marshall bodies, and 20 Daimler Fleetline double-deckers with Park Royal bodies. New deliveries in 1970 were Reliances with Duple and Plaxton coach bodies. East Kent was unique among NBC fleets, and unusual among larger fleets in Britain at the time, in that it didn't use fleetnumbers for its buses and coaches; these were known by registration numbers only, but secondhand acquisitions occasionally caused complications.

During 1970 it withdrew older types – Guy Arab II, III and IV models, as well as rarer types like Dennis Lancet J3s and Lancet UF coaches.

East Kent was also involved in coaching work, with one-third of its 1970 fleet classified as coaches, many of them working on the regular services to London from Canterbury, Dover, Folkestone, Herne Bay, Margate and Ramsgate.

The present-day successor to East Kent is Stagecoach in East Kent and Hastings, which operates some 300 vehicles.

West of the East Kent area was Maidstone & District Motor Services, a company with its roots in a 1908 operation. In the 1930s it absorbed the Chatham tramway system and the Hastings trolleybus system, maintaining separate identities for these operations until the 1950s.

Wedged between East Kent, London Transport and Southdown, M&D provided substantial networks in the Medway Towns, Tunbridge Wells, Hastings, Bexhill and around Maidstone itself, where the company was based. Its situation meant that it operated many joint routes with its neighbours, including services to Brighton and Eastbourne with Southdown, and to Canterbury and Folkestone with East Kent.

The 1970 M&D fleet totalled 766 vehicles, including nearly 200 coaches, a reflection of the importance of coaching work to M&D and its former BET neighbours. M&D had regular

In addition to its large fleet of Park Royal-bodied AEC Regent Vs, East Kent bought three Bridgemasters in 1962.
Photobus

One of the attractive Park Royal-bodied Daimler Fleetlines delivered to East Kent in 1969.
Photobus

services to London from towns in its area like Bexhill, Gillingham, Hastings, Maidstone, Rye, Sheerness and Tenterden.

The M&D single-deck fleet in 1970 mainly comprised AEC Reliances with standard BET-style bodies from mainstream suppliers like Marshall, Park Royal, Willowbrook and Weymann as well as locally-built bodies from Beadle and Harrington. Leyland single-deckers bought in the 1960s were Willowbrook-bodied Leopards and substantial batches of Leyland's rear-engined Panther with Strachans or Willowbrook bodies.

The double-deck fleet had been dominated by Leyland for some years and in 1959 M&D famously bought some early production Atlanteans; over 140 MCW-bodied examples were delivered between 1959 and 1963 before the company changed to Daimler Fleetlines, receiving more than 70 Northern Counties-bodied examples between 1963 and 1968.

The coach fleet was mainly AEC Reliance, often with Harrington bodies.

In 1970 M&D received the first of several batches of shorter Leyland Leopard PSU4s, these ones with Marshall bodies, Marshall-bodied two-door Daimler Fleetline single-deckers, and Leopard/Duple coaches. Withdrawals included all of its Leyland Titan PD2/12s, Albion Nimbuses, and AEC Reliances and Regent Vs.

In 1995 M&D was sold to British Bus, and survives as part of the 680-vehicle Arriva Southern Counties operation, still based in Maidstone.

West of M&D was one of the most popular bus operators in Britain, Brighton-based Southdown Motor Services, which operated along the south coast from Eastbourne to Portsmouth,

with routes stretching north across the downs towards London Transport territory and connecting with Maidstone & District to the east. Coaching was an important element of the Southdown business, including the comprehensive network of long-distance services into London and a significant day and extended tour business.

Like East Kent, it was formed by an amalgamation of pioneer bus companies, in 1915, expanding in the 1920s and 1930s and rationalising its strong position with co-ordination agreements with the municipal operators at Portsmouth and Brighton. In 1969 management of another NBC company, the former Tilling Group Brighton Hove & District, had passed into Southdown management. BH&D was formed by Tilling when it acquired the town routes of the Brighton Hove & Preston United company; the country routes passed to Southdown. The BH&D fleet consisted entirely of double-deck Bristols for a number of years, but in 1968 it bought Bristol RESL6G single-deckers with two-door ECW bodies.

More than four in every five 'pure' Southdown buses in 1970 was a Leyland, including the famous fleet of Northern Counties-bodied Titan PD3 'Queen Marys' and a sizeable fleet of Leopard buses and coaches.

New deliveries to the Southdown-BH&D fleet in 1970 included Duple-bodied Leopard coaches, plus two types that introduced Bristols to the Southdown fleet, other than the

Left: After its substantial fleet of Regent Vs, East Kent turned to Daimler Fleetlines in 1969 when it bought 20 of these attractive Park Royal-bodied 72-seaters, as seen in Margate. They pioneered a body style that would become particularly popular throughout the 1970s from a range of builders.
Tony Wilson

Centre: East Kent was also involved in the popular services linking London with the south-east coast, often using Park Royal-bodied AEC Reliances like this early 36ft-long example, new in 1962 and seen at Victoria Coach Station, London, with South Midland and United Counties coaches in the background.
Tony Wilson

Below: Later East Kent Regent Vs had more conventional, rather less attractive Park Royal bodies, like this 1962 example seen in Canterbury. The lack of a fleetnumber is apparent; East Kent relied on registration numbers.
Tony Wilson

absorbed BH&D buses; these were RESLs with Marshall bodies and VRTs with ECW bodies. There were also Northern Counties-bodied Daimler Fleetlines – but the Leyland name would return to Southdown with the delivery of Atlanteans and Nationals during the 1970s. On order for 1971 were 15 long Fleetlines and 25 Leopard/Plaxton coaches. Withdrawals in 1970 included Tiger Cubs and Titans, including Queen Marys, Beadle-Commer coaches and Guy Arab IVs, some of which were exported to China Motor Bus, Hong Kong.

Southdown and BH&D were separated again in 1985 prior to the NBC privatisation, and although both parts were sold to management-led teams, they were sold again – Southdown to Stagecoach in 1989 and what had been renamed Brighton & Hove to Go-Ahead Group in 1993. Today what was Southdown is part of the Stagecoach South operation, while Brighton & Hove thrives as a 252-vehicle operation, roundly 100 more than in the 1970 BH&D fleet.

Four municipal bus operators served south-east towns in 1970.

Maidstone Corporation was the smallest, with just 46 buses. It had opened an electric tramway in 1904, replaced it with trolleybuses between 1928 and 1930, and from 1924 started buying motorbuses, which finally replaced the trolleybuses in 1967. The 1970 fleet consisted of Massey-bodied Leylands, Titans and Atlanteans, and the unusual light brown/cream fleet livery was being replaced by a pale blue/ivory scheme introduced with the first Atlanteans in 1965.

More Atlanteans would be bought in the early 1970s, but the undertaking moved on to single-deckers. The fleet livery changed again during the 1980s, and the name Boro'line Maidstone was adopted in 1986, but financial problems led to the sale of the business to Maidstone & District in 1992.

Heading west along the south coast, Eastbourne Corporation is next. Never a tramway operator, Eastbourne introduced a very early motorbus service, in 1903. The 53 buses in the fleet in 1970 were AECs, Daimlers and Leylands; there were Regent

and Titan double-deckers, many with East Lancs bodies, although in the late-1960s Eastbourne had bought various rear-engined single-deckers, all with East Lancs two-door bodies; there were Daimler Roadliners and Leyland Panthers, and a former Panther Cub/Strachans demonstrator.

New deliveries in 1970 were East Lancs-bodied Panthers, and seven Atlanteans were ordered. Withdrawals included the first Regent V to leave the fleet.

Eastbourne Buses is one of Britain's surviving bus fleets in local authority ownership, with 66 buses in 2005.

Brighton Corporation had 62 buses in 1970. It started operating electric trams in 1901, and closed the system in 1939 when it changed over to municipal motorbuses and trolleybuses. A co-ordination agreement with the Brighton Hove & District bus company introduced BH&D buses and trolleybuses on agreed routes; the BH&D fleet wore the corporation red/cream colours

without the municipal coat of arms. Trolleybus operation ceased in 1961 and in the early 1970s a blue/white livery was adopted.

Brighton's 1970 all-Leyland bus fleet was mainly Titan double-deckers with MCW forward entrance bodies, and in the early 1970s Willowbrook and East Lancs-bodied Atlanteans would be bought.

In 1997 what had become Brighton Blue Bus was bought by Go-Ahead Group and subsequently absorbed into its Brighton & Hove company.

The furthest west of the municipal fleets covered by this book was the City of Portsmouth Passenger Transport Department, which was also the largest, with 180 buses in 1970. The corporation started in 1901 and immediately started to convert acquired horse tramways to electric operation. It bought motorbuses from 1919 and trolleybuses replaced the trams between 1934 and 1936; trolleybuses were withdrawn in 1963.

Left: East Kent converted buses to open-top layout for seafront services and these were popular at Epsom on Derby Day. This is a 1952 Guy Arab IV/Park Royal.
B W Spencer

Below: The last East Kent Regent V/Park Royals were ungainly from any angle, as this official view of a 1967 delivery reveals.
Park Royal

Maidstone & District maintained a smart coaching fleet, including this 1968 Duple Commander-bodied Leyland Leopard PSU3A/4RT.
Photobus/P Sykes/OTA

A Maidstone & District Leyland Leopard PSU3A/4RT of 1968, with Willowbrook 49-seat body, at Victoria Coach Station in May 1969.
Edward Shirras

A Joint Transport Area was set up in 1948 with Southdown, leading to an integrated service network.

The 1970 fleet was largely MCW-bodied Leylands, Titans and Atlanteans, but with an increasing single-deck fleet – Weymann-bodied Tiger Cubs and Leopards then Marshall and MCW-bodied Panther Cubs and Marshall-bodied AEC Swifts. More Atlanteans and Panthers were ordered during 1970 and withdrawals included the last of the Leyland-bodied Titan PD2/10s. In 1970 Portsmouth was still operating its famous fleet of four 1935 English Electric-bodied open-top Leyland Titan TD4s, but this would be their last season, though all would be bought for preservation.

The local authority sold its transport business to a consortium led by Southampton Citybus in 1988, then to Stagecoach, which was forced to sell it on, this time to Transit Holdings. FirstBus then bought it in 1996, merging what had become Portsmouth Transit with its People's Provincial company.

At the extreme western end of the area covered by this book was one of the more unusual operations – the Gosport & Fareham Omnibus Co Ltd, better-known by its Provincial fleetname. This had started as a tramway company, with buses replacing the trams in 1929. It had remained independent of the big groups for many years, and was noted for its distinctive vehicle-buying policies, with elderly AECs running into the 1960s alongside Guy Arabs, some fitted with Deutz air-cooled engines.

During 1970 Provincial was bought over by NBC and its quirky fleet replaced by buses drafted in from other group companies. The Provincial Bus Company was sold in 1987 to an equal co-ownership of employees and quickly renamed People's Provincial. It was bought by FirstBus in 1995. ∎

After its Leopards Southdown moved on to the Bristol RE, in RESL and RELL versions. This RELL6G with 49-seat Marshall body is seen in Old Steine, Brighton, with an early imported Mercedes-Benz 0302 coach from the Seamarks, Luton fleet on the right.
Geoff O'Brien

Brighton Hove & District had passed into Southdown control when this 1961 Bristol FSF6G with 60-seat ECW body was photographed at Whitehawk late in 1969. Note the unusual nearside route number display.
Ted Jones

Maidstone & District was an early customer for the Leyland Atlantean, taking 50 in 1959, mainly to replace the Hastings trolleybuses. Most were normal-height buses, but 14 had Weymann semi-lowbridge bodies like this one in Bexhill in November 1969.
Ted Jones

The first of Maidstone & District's semi-lowbridge Weymann-bodied Leyland Atlanteans is seen in Eastbourne heading for Hastings.
Tony Wilson

A vivid illustration of what was to come in NBC fleets when traditional liveries were replaced by NBC standard schemes. The normal-height Atlantean on the left is in traditional Maidstone & District livery, although with NBC-style fleetnames, while the AEC Reliance/Willowbrook on the right is in NBC leaf green with white relief.
Photobus

Another contrast of traditional and NBC liveries – a 1965 Maidstone & District AEC Reliance 2U3RA with Weymann 49-seat body at Brighton in 1974 beside an NBC-liveried Southdown Bristol RELL6G/Marshall.
Mark Page

Above: In addition to its Willowbrook-bodied Leyland Panther PSUR1/1Rs Maidstone & District bought Strachans-bodied 48-seaters like this example.

Photobus/P Sykes/OTA

Below: Southdown's Marshall-bodied Bristol RELL6Gs still retained the character of this popular company. This 1969 example is seen at Crawley.

Edward Shirras

Above: The Southdown Queen Mary Northern Counties-bodied Leyland Titan PD3/4s underwent a touch of modernisation with the final deliveries. A curved glass upper screen and panoramic side windows distinguish this 1967 example from earlier batches.

Edward Shirras

Left: A 1962 Brighton Hove & District Bristol FS6G with a convertible open-top ECW body running in 1971 on the 17 Portslade-Rottingdean seafront service.

A Swain

Above: During the 1960s Maidstone Corporation changed its livery from a distinctive light brown to the blue/cream style worn by this 1959 Leyland Titan PD2/20 with 61-seat Massey body.
Geoff O'Brien

Left: Between 1965 and 1968 Maidstone bought Leyland Atlantean PDR1/1s with Massey 74-seat bodies, like this one crossing Maidstone Bridge.
Ted Jones

Eastbourne Corporation was another south coast municipality that changed liveries, abandoning this blue/primrose scheme in favour of a simpler cream livery. This 1956 AEC Regent V in the older livery late in 1969 has East Lancs bodywork.
Ted Jones

Above: In the later Eastbourne livery, a 1968 Leyland Panther PSUR1/1R with 45-seat East Lancs two-door body at Grand Parade in November 1969.
Ted Jones

Below: In 1970 Brighton Corporation abandoned the traditional red/cream colours its buses had shared with those of Brighton Hove & District, in favour of this pale blue/white scheme. Brighton was a pioneer of driver-only double-deckers using what some operators would regard as unsuitable vehicles, front-engined halfcab double-deckers like this 1961 Leyland Titan PD2/37 with 64-seat Weymann body seen on Marine Parade.
Ted Jones

Top: Ordered by Brighton Hove & District but delivered to
Southdown in 1969, a Bristol VRTSL6G with ECW 70-seat body.
M A Penn

Below: A batch of 10 Daimler Fleetline/Northern Counties two-
door 74-seaters were delivered to Southdown in BH&D red/cream
in 1969/70.

Above: One of Maidstone Corporation's 1961 Massey-bodied Leyland Titan PD2A/30s pulls out to pass a Maidstone & District Daimler Fleetline.
Photobus

Below: A 1968 Leyland Atlantean PDR1/1 of Maidstone Corporation with the rather square style of Massey body fitted to rear-engined chassis, contrasting with the bodybuilder's rounded designs on earlier types.
B D Nicholson

Above: Brighton Corporation bought examples of the rare Leyland Panther Cub in 1969, fitted with Strachans bodywork.
Mark Page

Below: The October 1969 late autumn sun catches a Portsmouth City 1957 Leyland Titan PD2/40 with Weymann Orion-style 56-seat body, complete with unusual half-drop windows.
Ted Jones

Above: After standardising largely on double-deckers, City of
Portsmouth went for single-deckers in the late-1960s, returning to
double-deckers in the 1970s. In October 1969 a 1967 Leyland
Panther Cub PSRC1/1 with Metro-Cammell 42-seat two-door body
is seen at Hilsea.

Ted Jones

Below: Another late-1960s City of Portsmouth single-decker, a
1969 AEC Swift 2MP2R with Marshall 42-seat two-door body is
seen at Southsea.

Mark Page

Above: A 1966 Eastbourne Corporation Leyland Titan PD2A/30 with East Lancs 60-seat body featuring deep upper deck windows and a plethora of opening windows and ventilators. It is seen in July 1970. W T Cansick

Below: Eastbourne bought this East Lancs-bodied Daimler Roadliner SRC6 in 1967, and bought another two the following year.

Above: Like so many other fleets in this book, Brighton Corporation specified two-door bodies for new deliveries in the late 1960s, though most reverted to the single door layout. This is a 1969 Strachans-bodied two-door Leyland Panther Cub.
Photobus

Below: Two Brighton Leyland Titan PD2/37s with Weymann 64-seat forward entrance bodies at the Old Steine; the bus on the left wears the former red/cream livery and the other the newer blue/white scheme.
M P M Nimmo

Above: Although still in independent ownership when this photograph was taken, Provincial would pass into NBC ownership in 1970 and its quirky fleet was quickly replaced. This 1952 Guy Arab with Guy bodywork is seen in November 1970 in West Street, Fareham.
Ted Jones

Left: One of Provincial's full-fronted Guy Arabs with Provincial/Reading bodywork, a former London Transport 1946 Arab II with a 1965 body, seen in October 1969.
Ted Jones